Decoupage
IN A WEEKEND

Decoupage

IN A WEEKEND

Original ideas for over 50
quick and easy designs

JULIET BAWDEN

NH
NEW
HOLLAND

Happy 40th Birthday Caroline

First published in 1996 by
New Holland (Publishers) Ltd
London • Cape Town • Sydney • Singapore

24 Nutford Place,London W1H 6DQ,United Kingdom

80 McKenzie Street,Cape Town 8001,South Africa

3/2 Aquatic Drive,Frenchs Forest, NSW 2086,Australia

Reprinted 1997

ISBN 1 85368 724 3 (hb)
ISBN 1 85368 725 1 (pb)

Editor: Emma Callery
Designer: Peter Crump
Photographer: Shona Wood
Cover ilustration: Labeena Ishaque

Editorial direction: Yvonne McFarlane

Reproduction by Hirt and Carter (Pty) Ltd
Printed and bound by Times Offset (M) Sdn. Bhd.

Author's acknowledgement
I would like to thank the following people for their help in making
this book: my assistant Labeena Ishaque for all her hard work,
Shona Wood for her wonderful photography, and my publisher,
Yvonne McFarlane, for allowing me to create the book.

Important: Every effort has been made to present clear and accurate
instructions Therefore, the author and publishers can accept no liability for
any injury, illness or damage which may inadvertently be caused to
the user whilst following these instructions.

CONTENTS

INTRODUCTION

If you wish to take up a new craft, what could be easier than decoupage, as it really can be done anywhere? All you need are fine-pointed scissors — nail scissors will do the job very well — and PVA glue, which works both as an adhesive and as a varnish. Decoupage is one of those crafts which can be done in stages. So, if you want to, you can cut out motifs while watching the television or listening to the radio. The motifs can come from old magazines, greetings cards, wrapping paper, stamps, and jar labels, or you can cut or tear coloured paper into any shape you fancy. Once the motifs are ready, you will then only need a surface on which to decoupage which can be something as mundane as a shoe box or old sweet tin, or indeed any other container found about the house. Unlike painting, you don't need to be skilful, just careful.

With decoupage, you can achieve very sophisticated results from humble materials. In this book, for example, I have stuck motifs onto the inside of glass containers and then covered the whole interior with a coat of emulsion paint for a lovely translucent finish (see pages 62-3).

Or, by cutting out cat silhouettes from black sugar paper, I have transformed a plain white lampshade into a sophisticated shade fit for any cat lover (see pages 42-3). Both of these projects were incredibly quick to prepare and finish — just what is needed for a weekend's craft activity.

Decoupage is a great way of renewing items that look old, tired or scruffy. Among these pages you will find glass bottles, flowerpots, wooden hooks, a doll's crib, candlesticks and a window wedge — look around your home and almost anything you set your eyes on can be covered in decoupage in one way or another. Even walls and doors can be decorated with this technique. Look in boot fairs and thrift shops for other items to decoupage such as chairs, tables, cupboards small and large, old wooden boxes and mirror frames.

Once you start working with decoupage, you may well find that it is one of those crafts that you won't want to stop. Also, because its essential materials such as emulsion or acrylic paints and PVA glue dry so quickly, decoupage really is the ideal weekend craft.

Juliet Bawden

GETTING STARTED

Decoupage is the art of decorating a surface with scraps or cutouts of printed images. It is a very straightforward process: select an image which is then carefully cut out, glue it to the chosen object and then varnish. It is a pastime that can be enjoyed by both adults and children alike and some stunning effects can be produced. Tired household items such as boxes, picture frames, candlesticks, watering cans, vases and endless other objects can be easily decorated using decoupage.

HISTORY OF DECOUPAGE

The French verb découper means 'to cut out' and decoupage is the term now applied internationally to this craft which can be traced back to the time when paper was first introduced in the twelfth and thirteenth centuries.

Throughout this period, paper cutouts were used in Europe but the art of decoupage as we know it today, really had its origins in the late seventeenth century in Italy. It was at this time that there was a love for chinoiserie (objects or furniture decorated in the Chinese style). These were usually hand-painted and highly lacquered and there was an enormous demand, especially in Venice. In order to keep abreast with the quantities required, a new technique was introduced to imitate lacquer ware and this was decoupage. The whole process was considerably reduced in cost through copying the original piece of furniture by making it in papier mâché. This would then be covered in gesso, which in turn would have hand-tinted prints pasted to the surface which craftsmen had mass-produced from

their original designs. Finally, the furniture would have up to 30 coats of varnish applied so that the object would emulate the original lacquered furniture which came from the Orient. This art form became more popular than the very one it was trying to imitate and became known as Art Provo.

Meanwhile, in Britain, another form of decoupage was developing due to a thriving papier mâché industry and this was known as japanning. Many of the designs were similar to the original Chinese lacquer work, but the quality was thought to be superior and they were applied to papier mâché, wood, leather and tin. There was a wealth of material published during the eighteenth century using different methods such as engraving and etching, which had long been established, stone lithographs, aquatints and mezzotints, providing the decoupeur with a wide choice of subject matter.

At the beginning of the nineteenth century, purpose-made scraps first appeared which were usually black and white engravings that were often tinted. These then became more elaborate and were sometimes embossed, giving a three-dimensional

appearance to the object. The printing and embossing processes by which these were manufactured soon became automated, which meant that the volume of available scraps increased tremendously, and during the Victorian period these became an integral part of various pastimes.

Precut scraps also started to be produced so that the laborious task of cutting out every image was removed. The subject matter was usually sentimental and romantic, with angels, fans, flowers, well-dressed ladies and angelic children being the most well-liked. Military and naval themes were also very popular and scraps were used to cover entire surfaces of trunks, boxes, tins and trays.

Queen Victoria was an avid collector of scraps, as were children of the period for whom special editions of cutouts were introduced, featuring nursery rhyme characters, fairy tales, animals and alphabets. A wide range of seasonal scraps were also produced, for example celebrating Christmas, with Santa Claus being much favoured, together with angels, children and winter scenes.

Decoupage remained popular in Germany, France (where these cutouts were called 'chromos'), and America where they were known as 'swags'.

In the early twentieth century, the editor of Paris *Vogue*, Caroline Duer, was responsible for the American interest as she produced some particularly fine examples of decoupage which can still be seen today. She worked, with great panache in the mid-nineteenth-century German Biedermeier style, using gold braid, paper, flowers and embossed paper.

The huge increase in interest for decoupage during the last few years means that these scraps still sell well despite the fact that there is a vast array of materials which can be utilized to create some interesting work. Magazines, posters, packaging, postcards, used cards, wrapping paper and the use of the photocopy machine to copy, enlarge and reduce in size thousands of images means that today it is possible to create a contemporary piece of attractive decoupage very easily in the home in a weekend.

WHAT YOU WILL NEED

You will probably find that you have a lot of the equipment for decoupage lying around your home but if not, most of those things that are necessary are inexpensive and fairly widely available.

BRUSHES

Paintbrushes come in a variety of widths and so the area of the surface being painted will determine the size needed. It is advisable to buy the best quality you can afford as work can be ruined by stray hairs being caught in paint or varnish. These brushes are particularly suitable for oil-based paints and varnish but can obviously be used for many purposes. Artist's brushes are useful for hand-tinting prints and if acrylic paint is to be used. It is advisable to keep brushes separate once used. Use white spirit to clean your brushes unless water-based paints are being used in which case ordinary water will clean them successfully.

GLUES

• **PVA GLUE** This glue is sometimes referred to as white glue and is inexpensive. It dries reasonably quickly and has a clear finish. It can be watered down and also used as a varnish.

• **SPRAY ADHESIVES** These are very clean, fast to use and do allow some movement when first applied to the object. They must be used in a well-ventilated room and directed carefully over a piece of scrap paper ①.

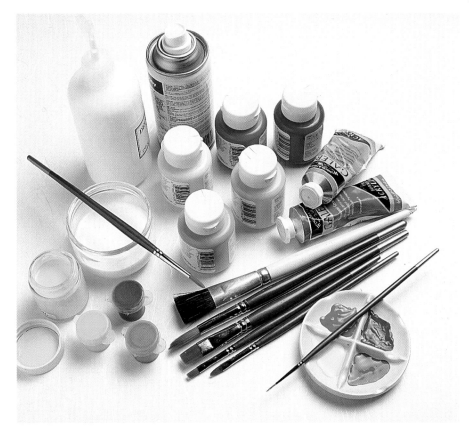

• **WALLPAPER PASTE** This is a slower drying glue than PVA and so has the advantage of allowing you to alter the position of the image if necessary. It also allows more time for smoothing out any wrinkles that may occur and is very cheap.

• **WOOD GLUE** Use when applying motifs to wooden surfaces.

METHYLATED SPIRITS

This can be used with wire wool (see overleaf) when preparing the surface of an object and it is also useful for removing any excess polish. Methylated spirits can be added to shellac to dilute it and it is useful for cleaning brushes.

OBJECTS SUITABLE FOR DECOUPAGE

The starting point for decoupage is the choice of object you wish to decorate and this can be of any age and be made from a variety of materials, as long as the surface is hard. Decoupage can give a new lease of life to many old, shabby-looking items such as tea caddies, biscuit tins, trays, vases, bowls, boxes, etc. Likewise, a paper surface such as a shoe or chocolate box presents no problems, and metal surfaces are very

successful too — jugs, plates, buckets and empty tins. Furniture, floors, walls and doors are a challenge as the area to cover is obviously larger, but the end result is very effective. It is also fun to go into junk shops to find objects to decoupage, or you can buy new containers such as boxes, tins, picture frames ② and small chests. Occasionally there are advertisements in women's magazines for hat boxes, and your local hardware store is likely to have quite a supply of galvanized metal containers such as watering cans, buckets, coal scuttles and enamelled, wooden or terracotta objects.

PAPER SEALERS

The quality of the paper that you may use to decoupage with will vary enormously, and some papers may bleed or discolour before being applied to the surface of an object if it is not sealed first. The use of a sealant, then, will prevent discolouration and make the image very much easier to handle. Wait for the sealant to dry before cutting out the images.

- **SHELLAC OR A WHITE FRENCH POLISH** Use these products to cover an image before it is cut out. Shellac will make the paper transparent when first applied but will dry to a clear finish. French polish is also sometimes sold as button polish.
- **PRINT FIXATIVE SPRAY** This may be used as a sealant, resulting in a rubber-based coating.

PAINTS

To a certain extent, the object selected for decoupage will dictate which paint to use, but it is worth noting that water-based paints are easier to use. Oil-based paints usually produce a more brilliant colour and can be thinned with the use of white spirit to make them easier to use, but they are also more expensive to buy.

- **ACRYLIC PAINTS** These are quick drying, water-based and can be applied over emulsion or oil-based paints. They produce very strong colours and are available in little tins or tubes from craft shops. Once the decoupage has been applied, acrylic paint is useful to add extra decoration.
- **ARTIST'S OIL PAINTS** These are expensive and should be used sparingly just to add tints with crackle glaze.
- **EMULSION PAINTS** These water-based paints can be thinned by adding water and are relatively quick drying. Several coats will need to be applied and they make a good base for decoupage.
- **GLOSS PAINTS** These are oil-based and come in a matt, eggshell or gloss finish. They can be thinned with white spirit and give a tougher finish. Twenty-four hours should be left between coats.
- **METAL PAINTS** These come in a wide range of colours and are best used on metal surfaces.

- **PRIMER** New and stripped wooden surfaces will need a coat of primer to prevent the paint from being absorbed into the grain. New metal objects will also need priming either with a red oxide or special metal primer which can easily be purchased from a decorator's shop ③.
- **UNDERCOAT** Undercoat should be used on primed, unvarnished wood.

RESOURCES FOR SCRAPS AND CUTOUTS

There is a vast array of printed material available to the decouper today but it will take a little time to build up a supply. It is advisable to save anything you come across which you find attractive so that when the right object comes along you have your own resources to draw upon. It is a good idea to have several different folders or boxes so that when you decide to keep a scrap it can be filed under, say, flowers, cherubs, sea/shells, or any other area of your choice.

It is useful to keep postcards, Christmas and birthday cards, gift wrapping, magazines, catalogues and manuals. A good supply can be found in museums and galleries where you may also come across old charts, drawings, sketches and even old books. Books are a wonderful resource and images can be photocopied in black and white as well as colour and can be enlarged or reduced in size.

The original Victorian scraps are regularly reproduced and these can be obtained by mail order, although many can also be found in museum and craft shops. Traditionally, black and white images were used for decoupage and these were sometimes hand-tinted; take

colour photocopies if this is your only supply. It is worth remembering that there can be a greyness if using a photocopy, so be careful to select the correct paint.

ROLLERS

These are useful for rolling over the glued paper once it is in position on the surface. It ensures there is no trapped air, removes any excess glue and irons out any wrinkles. Alternatively, use your fingers for smaller areas, or a clean, soft cloth.

SANDPAPER AND WIRE WOOL

These are needed when preparing a surface before gluing begins and for sanding down paint and varnish between coats. Both abrasives are available in several grades ranging from fine to coarse.

SCALPEL OR CRAFT KNIFE

These are necessary for cutting a straight line, border or any intricate detail. It is important that the blade is sharp and is replaced if there is a nick or it is blunt, or the edge of the image that is being cut will be rough. It is useful to have a special cutting mat ④ when using a scalpel, but a thick piece of card will protect a surface if this is not possible.

SCISSORS

You will need the sharpest pair of manicure scissors you can find and the better the quality the easier the cutting will be. It does not matter if the scissors have a straight or curved blade ④.

WATERCOLOURS AND COLOURED PENCILS

The easiest way to colour a print which has been reproduced in black and white is to use watercolours or coloured pencils. Watercolours can be bought very cheaply and layers of colour can be built up making sure each layer is thoroughly dry before the next is applied. To paint with a single colour, use different depths of the same colour, starting with a thin wash over the complete image. More colour can then be added and the lighter areas painted, and so on until the darkest areas of the image are painted with the colour plus a little added black.

Likewise, when using coloured pencils, gradually build up the image, lightly shading to begin with and then creating more of a density as you proceed. Once you have finished, cover all the pencil work with a beige coloured pencil to blend the whole surface together.

VARNISHES

• **ACRYLIC VARNISH** This is more expensive than ordinary varnish but will not yellow with age and is available with a matt or gloss finish.

• **COLOURED VARNISH** An aged look can be created using oak or antique pine varnishes. The varnish needs to be applied and then rubbed off, leaving a residue behind.

• **CRACKLE VARNISH** This gives the work an ancient, cracked look. Use two varnishes which work against each other so that one dries slowly and the other rapidly, (see also page 13).

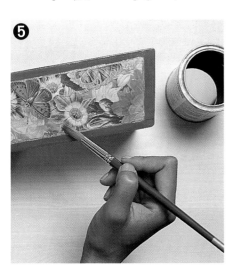

• **POLYURETHANE CLEAR WOOD VARNISH** This can be bought from decorator's suppliers and comes in clear, yellow and tinted shades. It has different finishes so that it can give a high gloss, satin or matt effect ⑤, depending on which you favour, and if painted over all of the object it will give a lasting finish to your decoupage.

WAX

Waxing is the final coat given to the decoupaged surface and is available as beeswax as well as a number of other finishes. It should only be applied when the surface is completely dry. The first coat should be thick and left for a couple of hours before being polished followed by one or two thinner coats.

WOOD FILLERS

It is good to have a quick drying wood filler to hand. It fills cracks, rough surfaces and small holes.

PREPARATION OF SURFACES

The first stage with decoupage is the preparation of the surface and although this may be tedious it is worth doing well as it can affect the quality of the finished item tremendously.

CERAMIC

Ceramic surfaces are ideal for working on but you must ensure that they are dust free. New terracotta pots or plaques can be lightly sanded and sealed with a water-based varnish which will provide the key for adhesive.

METAL

Old metal that has rust on must be treated otherwise the rust will eventually reappear and spoil the finished decoupage. Rub down flaking and loose metal and then remove it with a wire brush, heavy duty steel wool or coarse sandpaper ①. The object should then be washed with a solution of half vinegar and half water and thoroughly dried. To ensure the piece remains rust-free, prime the surface with two coats of rust-resistant

paint or a red oxide. You can buy an all-in-one rust-proofer and primer and in this case follow the manufacturer's instructions.

New metal should always be washed either with water and detergent or with the vinegar and water solution mentioned above. The metal surface must then be thoroughly dry before applying the two coats of red oxide or an oil-based primer. This procedure must be followed for enamel, tin or any galvanized metal objects being prepared for decoupage.

WOOD

Old wood must be sanded and cleaned thoroughly whether it has been painted, varnished or waxed. Clean the surface with detergent and water and fill any holes with a wood filler. When dry, sand the object with a medium grade sandpaper so that the surface is completely smooth.

When stripping a piece of furniture or object completely, you can always go to a commercial wood stripper but if you prefer to do the stripping yourself, buy a bottle of paint stripper or try wire wool soaked in methylated or white spirit. Once the surface has been stripped and sanded, seal it with a coat of shellac or wood primer.

New wood can be sealed with a coat of primer or undercoat but if the grain of the wood and natural colour is important to the appearance, coat it with shellac. This must then be lightly sanded to provide a key for adhesive to stick easily.

PAINTING THE BACKGROUND

Many objects will need a base colour on which to be glued and at least two coats will be needed. Emulsion paint is ideal for covering the object you are working on and this can be diluted with a little water before being applied to the surface with a normal household paintbrush. After each coat, allow time for it to dry properly and sand lightly before applying the second layer. Oil-based paint can be used for this stage if you prefer and it is advisable if an object will get a lot of use as it will be less likely to chip than emulsion. Again it can be diluted, but this time with turpentine or white spirit.

CUTTING AND PREPARING THE SCRAPS

The surface of all paper used for decoupage must be sealed before cutting out as this will prevent discolouration and also make it much easier to cut delicate pieces (see paper sealers on page 10).

Cut out the scraps as accurately as possible with small sharp scissors ① and/or a scalpel or craft knife. Embroidery scissors are very good for particularly fiddly pieces. When using the scalpel or craft knife, place the image on a cutting mat so as not to damage the surface beneath ②. You will also need a larger pair of scissors to cut the paper into manageable sizes before cutting the more intricate parts of the image. Inevitably, all pictures

used will be printed on different weights of paper, but as a rule remember that the best results are achieved using paper that is as light as possible.

DESIGNING

When working on a flat object it is easy to place the cutout scraps on the surface and rearrange them until the whole composition is satisfactory. However, this is not always possible — especially when the surface is fixed and vertical or curved. When confronted with this situation, use reusable adhesive ③ or non-contact repositioning glue which will allow you to remove any images and alter their position. When you are satisfied with the composition, each image can be lifted and glued into place.

If you want to entirely cover a surface with motifs that overlap each other you will need to work out your design in a slightly different way. Start at the top and gradually work downwards. When the design feels right, make a note of the position of each scrap by taking a photograph or making a sketch. You can then remove the images, starting at the bottom and moving upwards so that the top pieces can be stuck into place first.

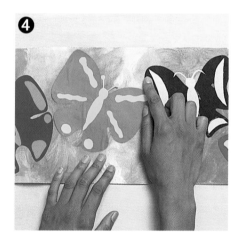

GLUING

The scraps can be stuck down permanently with either PVA or wallpaper paste. A paste allows more time for you to reposition an image if necessary as it is slower drying. The glue should always be applied to the surface of the object rather than the scrap as this is less messy and if the paper is a little fragile then less handling is involved. Press down the image firmly working outwards from the centre to remove any air bubbles ④. A roller may be a useful tool at this stage for eliminating air bubbles and it can help with any creasing that may have occurred.

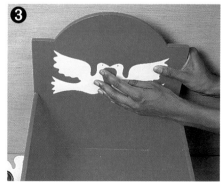

When the gluing has been completed, leave it to dry for half an hour before wiping any excess glue off the surface with a warm, wet cloth. However, if you are using PVA, wipe over the surface immediately as this adhesive dries hard. Occasionally wrinkles occur, particularly when the paper is extremely thin but these will disappear when everything is dry. Check that the edges do not begin to curl up while drying is taking place and if they do, apply a tiny amount of glue with a cocktail stick. When an air bubble does occur, pierce the bubble with a very sharp blade to allow the air to escape and then fill the incision with a small amount of glue. Leave the object to dry for a further two hours.

If you want to build up layers of decoupage to give a three-dimensional effect, paint on one layer of PVA adhesive to protect the work to date.

Leave to dry and then lightly sand over the surface ⑤. This may result in a white sheen but don't worry about it as subsequent layers of decoupage and PVA glue or varnish will cover it up. To finish the piece, tick on the next layer of decoupage, as before ⑥.

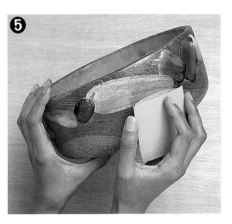

⑤

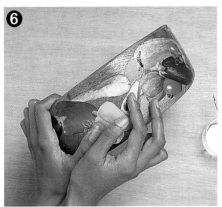

⑥

VARNISHING

When varnishing, you must always work in a dust-free, well-ventilated space. The brush used to apply the varnish should be of good quality so that hairs will not shed, spoiling the surface of the work.

Apply as many coats of varnish as you like from three up to twenty,

⑦

depending on the quality of finish that is desired. The first layer of varnish should be thin and applied evenly with a smooth finish ⑦. It should then be left for approximately two hours before brushing on the next layer. Varnishes dry quite rapidly these days so it is possible to put on four or five layers during the course of a day.

Lightly sand the penultimate coat although it is advisable not to do this unless at least six coats have been applied. The top layer can be shiny or matt depending on the finish desired. However, it is worth remembering that a matt varnish will give a cloudy appearance after two or three coats because of the matting agent.

FINISHING

Once the last coat of varnish has been applied the work is complete but if you want to achieve different finishes here are some further ideas with which to experiment.

ANTIQUING
An antique or brown staining wax can be applied with a soft cloth once varnishing has been completed and this will give a mellow look once the wax

has dried and been buffed with a clean cloth. An alternative method would be to make a solution with 1 part white emulsion, 3 parts raw umber pigment and 8 parts water which is brushed on after the second coat of varnish. Wait for a minute and then rub off with a paper towel or clean cloth. Once the surface is dry continue with the next layer of varnish.

CRACKLE VARNISH
Apply this to the top coat of varnish ⑧. The oil-based varnish is painted on first and allowed to dry before the water-based varnish is painted on top. When this is dry, the surface should look crazed but it may need a little help, in which case place the object near a lamp or radiator and this will encourage the cracking. Artist's oils, such as sienna or burnt umber, can be used to fill the cracks and are particularly effective.

WAXING
The application of several layers of wax will give a mellow and professional look to the decoupage. It works best on top of a matt varnish which should be rubbed down with a fine wire wool before applying the wax, as directed by the manufacturer's instructions.

⑧

CONTAINERS

From boxes to bins and cans to flowerpots, our homes are full of containers. As they are usually small they are good projects for starting on to practise the craft of decoupage. Many companies sell blank boxes especially for decoupage (see page 79), but why not collect your own containers and recycle them? Drinks, sweets or biscuits are frequently given in tins as presents — give them a coat of paint and then decoupage the exterior, or cover them entirely with images that obliterate any advertising. The most important thing is to end up with a container which is pleasing to you.

MEXICAN STORAGE BOX

This storage box is inspired by the colours of Mexico, the acid green and hot pink are a perfect foil for the piñata-style animals taken from gift wrapping paper. The decoupage is then further complemented by the hand-painted squiggles around the animals once they have been glued down. Adding painted details to a decoupaged item makes it even more original.

1 Paint the main part of the box with the pink emulsion and the lid with the green. Use two to three coats for each for a smooth finish, allowing the paint to dry in between coats.

VARIATIONS

If you know what you will be storing in your box before you cover it with decoupage, look for suitable motifs to stick on the outside such as books, toys or shoes. There are so many beautifully designed wrapping papers around these days that you are bound to find something that is just right.

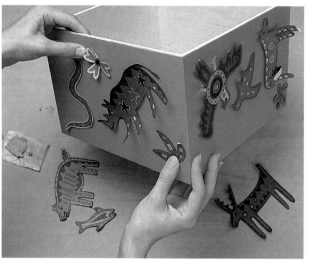

2 Choose your images from the wrapping paper and cut them out carefully, using either the pair of scissors or craft knife. For very fine work it is best to use embroidery scissors.

3 Arrange the images onto the box, once the paint is dry. Using the re-usable adhesive, re-arrange the images until you find the composition that you like.

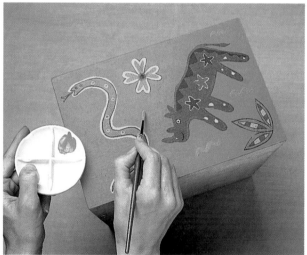

4 When you have decided on the composition, glue down the figures with PVA glue. Press down on each paper cutout firmly to get rid of any air bubbles.

5 Using the fine paintbrush and contrasting colour of emulsion, paint squiggles onto the box around the animals. Varnish with clear matt varnish, painting on as many coats as you wish, but allow each coat to dry before starting the next.

PAINTED HANDS DESIGN FOR A FILING BOX

By flicking through magazines and books you are sure to come across inspiring images to use in decoupage. The designs chosen for this filing box were found in a book on how to paint your hands with henna as do Indian brides. The patterns and hand shapes illustrated are so interesting and pretty that they were used here.

1 Paint the flat filing box with the white emulsion, using two to three coats for a smooth and even finish. Allow the paint to dry between each coat before applying the next

— VARIATIONS —

If you want a slightly softened design, consider colour-washing the hands before cutting them out — pale shades of pink and blue, say, will achieve a very pretty effect.

2 Cut out the hands and symbols from the henna pattern book or from your selected paper, using the scissors or the craft knife. Be very careful not to tear the fingers when cutting around them.

3 Arrange the hands around the flat box file, using the re-usable adhesive until you find a suitable composition. Here I positioned the hands to face each other so that the front and back of the box file would eventually be a mirror image of each other.

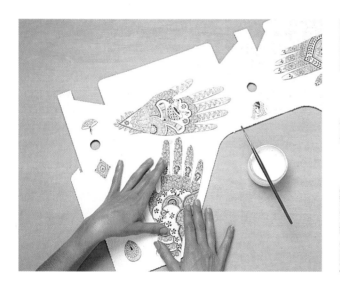

4 Stick down the paper images using a paintbrush to apply the PVA glue. Because the fingers are so fine, check that you put glue onto each one and then when you are sticking the hands in place run your fingers over the top to ensure no air bubbles are caught.

5 Varnish the flat box file with one or two coats of PVA glue. The glue will be white when you first apply it, but it will be transparent once it has dried.

SHELLS ON DISTRESSED FLOWERPOTS

Decoupage on a distressed surface is an unusual, yet striking way to disguise a set of inexpensive plastic flowerpots. These are the kinds of things that you will probably have hiding around the garden shed, but once they have been painted and covered with decoupage you will want to bring them out and show them off.

1 Paint each flowerpot with a couple of coats of white emulsion, making sure that the plastic surface is completely and quite thickly covered.

VARIATIONS

As the main photograph to the left indicates, you needn't feel limited to sticking on shell motifs to your flowerpots. Almost anything will do.— the vegetable etchings on the pot on the right would be perfect for vegetable seedlings, for example. But how about finding herbs for herb containers, or pansy motifs if you were going to grow them?

2 When the emulsion paint is dry, rub the polishing wax into the white surface using the soft cloth. Don't worry about getting an even coating, the wax will act as a resist for the next coat of emulsion paint giving the pot its distressed finish

3 With the blue emulsion, thickly paint over the waxed surface. Leave the pot to dry and then paint on a second coat of the blue emulsion, applying it just as thickly as the first.

4 When the blue paint has dried, scour over the flowerpot gently using the sponge to reveal sections of the white paint beneath it in a distressed style.

5 Before cutting out the shell images, paint them with a very diluted wash of blue acrylic paint and sweep over the images lightly with a wide paintbrush. Once the wash is dry, cut out the shells and then glue them down using the PVA glue making sure no air bubbles are left in place. Once you have done this, coat the flowerpot with as many layers of PVA glue as you wish. This acts like a water-based varnish. The more PVA, the shinier the finish will be.

MINI WINDOW BOX

As, more often than not, window boxes are used for growing colourful flowers throughout the summer, why not make an otherwise ordinary window box into something a little more floral? With the aid of some gift wrapping paper and gold paint, the flowery panels were very neatly defined on this box.

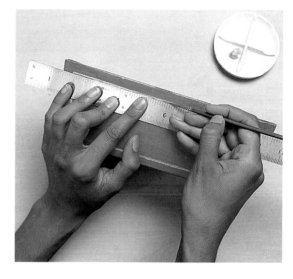

1 Prepare the window box for decoupage by painting the outside surface with the dark red emulsion paint. Paint two or three coats for a smooth and even finish, allowing each coat of paint to dry before applying the next. Paint a narrow strip in gold paint around the edge of each side to make a panel — use the metal ruler to help regulate the lines.

YOU WILL NEED

Small window box
Acrylic or emulsion paints (dark red, gold)
Paintbrushes (fine, medium)
Metal ruler
Scissors
Floral gift wrapping paper
PVA glue
Clear wood varnish
Sandpaper (fine)

— TIP —

Before buying the paint for decorating a window box like this, take a good look at the motifs you are going to be using and find a colour that really enhances them.

2 Carefully cut out your selected images from the floral gift wrapping paper, making sure that you cut enough to layer the images one over the other. Cut some of the flowers with straight edges so that they fit inside the gold line frame

3 Stick down the first layer with the PVA glue and then gently wipe over the top with your finger to get rid of the air bubbles. When the glue has dried, paint the flowers with clear wood varnish. Use six to seven coats, making sure that the previous coat has dried before you start on the next one.

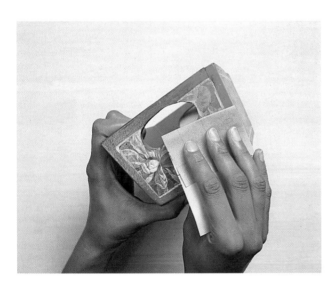

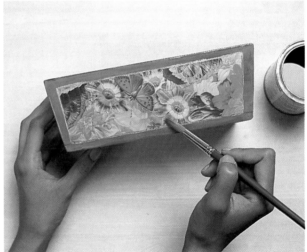

4 Using very fine grade sandpaper, sand over the varnished surface. You may find that the varnish will become opaque and white, but do not worry about this — step 5 will soon cover it up again.

5 Glue on the second layer of flowers in the same way as step 3, and then varnish again, once more using six or seven coats of clear wood varnish. You will see that the images from beneath will become clear again. If you wish to apply more layers, repeat steps 4 and 5 until your desired effect is achieved. Brush gold paint onto the top edges of the box to give a gold stained finish.

CONTAINERS GALLERY

Sheep box

Black line drawings of sheep have been enlarged on a photocopier and pasted onto a wooden salt box which has been painted with a dark green emulsion. Little tufts of grass were added in spring green and then the whole box was given four coats of acrylic varnish.

Heart-shaped box

A heart-shaped plywood box has been painted black and then decorated with golden suns and moons.

Wooden box (below)

This one is colourwashed in blue, and covered with images of the sea. It has been further decorated with embossed metal shapes made by drawing on the back of tomato purée tubes, and then cutting out using scissors.

Fishing box (right)

A plain plywood box has been decorated with fish for a keen fisherman friend. The fish have been cut out and then painted aquamarine and blue, and the box has been washed in blue. Two fish are painted red to add some contrast to the design.

Gift box

A box which originally contained a cake has been turned into a gift box by first painting it deep red. Images from a poster were photocopied and then the angels were cut out and touched on their rounded parts with a pink wash. The box was finally varnished with crackle varnish.

Corrugated box

Corrugated card has become rather fashionable, but it can be a little dull. The hexagonal box used here has been embellished using corrugated card hearts some of which have been sprayed gold.

Jewellery casket

This traditional jewellery casket was painted with coral coloured acrylic paint and then decorated with cutouts from a jeweller's catalogue. It was then painted with crackle varnish and burnt umber was rubbed into the cracks to make them show up.

GIFTS FOR THE HOME

Items for the home can include almost anything. For example, here I've decorated a tray with a glorious arrangement of flowers and butterflies. Previously, its varnish had been coming off but now it has been quite transformed. Then I took some old-fashioned kitchen scales, gave them a smart new coat of green paint and added Victorian scraps of flowers. Paper lampshades can be picked up from most major department stores and are easy to decoupage. Depending on how much light you wish to obliterate, make the pattern more or less dense.

TRELLIS CANDLESTICKS

Very delicate decoupage images can look stunning. The original concept of decoupage was to glue a cutout image onto a surface and then lacquer it until the image looked as if it was ingrained on the surface. So the more delicate or intricate the paper cutout, the more convincing the final article.

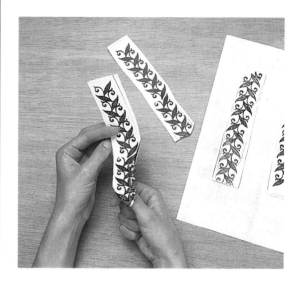

1 Photocopy your trellis design as many times as necessary. Then with the craft knife or manicure scissors (whichever you find most comfortable to use), carefully cut out the designs. Make sure the blade is sharp, otherwise it will be difficult to cut out the intricate swirls clearly and accurately. Also cut out a number of individual leaves.

YOU WILL NEED

Trellis design
Craft knife/manicure scissors
Acrylic paint (black)
Paintbrush (fine)
Re-usable adhesive
2 white ceramic candlesticks
PVA glue
Gloss varnish

VARIATIONS

Instead of positioning each piece of trellis so that it runs vertically up the candlesticks, try wrapping the trellis around the stem, winding up from the bottom to the top. You will need more pieces of trellis to achieve this, but the end result will look just like a piece of wrought iron.

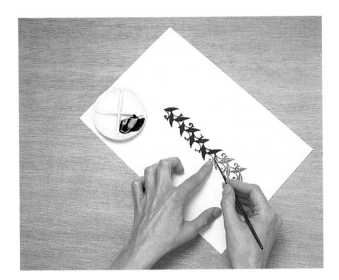

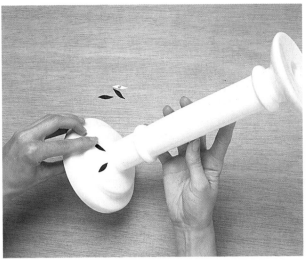

2 Lay the cutouts onto a piece of scrap paper and paint over them entirely with the black acrylic paint, using the fine paintbrush. This will make the colour denser on the design; black and white photocopies can sometimes look faded and grey. Allow the paint to dry.

3 Using the re-usable adhesive, arrange the individual leaves around the top and bottom edges of the candlesticks. It is ideal to use a re-usable adhesive as it is easy to keep on re-arranging the leaves until you find the right composition.

4 Use re-usable adhesive in the same way for the trellis strips along the stem of each candlestick. Then stick down each piece in its chosen position using the PVA glue.

5 Varnish the candlesticks with one or two coats of the gloss varnish to finish them off. You can use the PVA glue if you prefer. It will look opaque white when you first brush it on, but it will dry to a transparent finish.

TROMPE L'OEIL DRAWERS

A really fun way to decorate a set of drawers is to disguise them as an alternative storage space, such as stacked shelves. Having found some pictures in a magazine of towels, cushions and fabrics piled high, I cut them out and glued them onto the drawers.

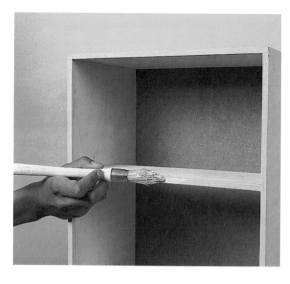

1 Remove the drawers from the surrounding unit and then paint the surround with the pale blue emulsion paint. Apply two to three coats for a smooth and even finish. Allow to dry between each coat, and again when finished.

YOU WILL NEED

Unit with wooden drawers
Emulsion paints (pale blue, various other colours to match the images)
Paintbrushes
Images taken from magazines
Ruler
Pencil
Scissors
PVA glue
Gloss varnish
Screw-in knobs

VARIATIONS

Instead of having a different design of decoupage on each drawer, take colour photocopies of your particular favourite and stick the same picture on each drawer to represent a much larger area of storage.

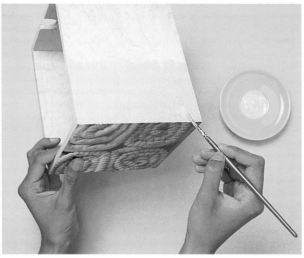

2 Select pictures from magazines: home interest magazines are the best bet for the type of images that have been chosen here. Measure the drawer fronts, then transfer those measurements to the back of the images using the ruler and pencil and cut out.

3 Paint the edges of each drawer to match the colours on the picture you have chosen to stick to that particular drawer. To finish off each drawer particularly neatly, you might choose to paint inside the drawers as well as outside.

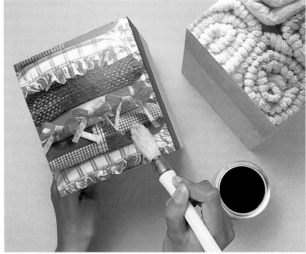

4 Stick down each picture onto the drawer face, wiping over the surface with a soft cloth to get rid of any air bubbles to ensure a smooth finish.

5 Varnish the decoupaged surfaces with two to three coats for a hard-wearing finish. Let each coat of varnish dry before applying the next one. To open each drawer with ease, screw a drawer knob into the centre of each one.

TROPICAL FISH BOTTLES

Water transfers are easy to apply and very effective, especially on the aquatic-like surface of blue glass. For coloured glass make sure that the fish transfers you choose are bright enough to be seen on the rather dark surface. If the contrast isn't good enough the bottles may look dull.

1 On the transfers there may be labels naming the fish — before you do anything else, cut these off otherwise you will get the writing on the bottle as well as the fish. Dip one transfer in the water and hold it there for a few seconds, until the design loosens on the paper.

YOU WILL NEED

Water transfers of fish

Scissors

Bowl of warm water

Blue glass bottle

Soft cloth

VARIATIONS

Instead of positioning the fish randomly around the bottle, you could create a shoal of fish by overlapping the transfers as they swim from one side of the bottle and disappear around a corner.

2 Place the paper holding the fish image face up on the area of the glass bottle where you have decided to place the transfer.

3 With the thumb of one hand, press gently on the top of the design to stop the fish transfer from moving about when you remove the backing paper.

4 Grasp the lower edge of the backing paper with your other hand and gently pull out the paper until the design is left free and in position.

5 Smooth out any water or air bubbles with the soft cloth. Then repeat steps 1 to 4 with other transfers until you have achieved the desired effect.

GALVANIZED TIN WATERING CAN

Covering tin ware with decoupage is a traditional form of this craft, and by making the images floral ones you will tie in the watering can very naturally with its surroundings in the garden. There are a great many floral gift wraps available from which you can cut your images.

1 If you need to, first use the wire wool to remove any rusty lumps that are on the outside of the watering can. Then wash the watering can thoroughly with warm water and detergent.

YOU WILL NEED

Galvanized watering can

Wire wool

Detergent

Metal primer

Paintbrushes

Turpentine

Gloss paint (dark green)

Floral images

Scissors

Re-usable adhesive

PVA glue

Clear varnish

— VARIATIONS —

Vegetables or gardening implements would be equally effective and suitable on a watering can such as this. Also, don't limit yourself to the watering can, how about applying decoupage to galvanized buckets or even an old tin bath if you can find one? The decorating principal is just the same.

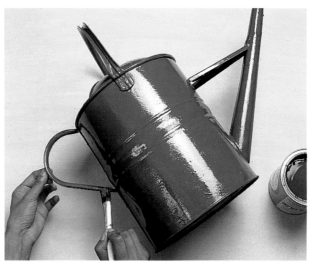

2 Once it is dry, paint the watering can with the metal primer. Be sure not to apply too thick a coat otherwise the surface on which you will decoupage may become uneven. Wash out the paintbrush thoroughly with the turpentine.

3 Once the primer is dry, paint the can all over with two coats of the dark green gloss paint, allowing the first coat to dry before you begin the next one.

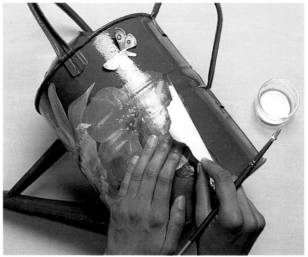

4 Cut out your chosen floral images using the scissors. The images should be quite large as smaller ones will not look as strong and clear. Arrange them on the dry watering can with the re-usable adhesive until you find a good composition.

5 Stick down the flowers with the PVA glue, pressing out the air bubbles as you go along. Stick down several layers to achieve a deeper look. Finally, apply between 10 and 12 coats of clear varnish to finish off.

STARS AND CIRCLES ROLLER BLIND

An unconventional way with which to decoupage is by using fabric. For this brightly coloured blind, gingham stars are attached to a fabric blind using fabric iron-on adhesive which makes it simple to make and also very effective.

1 Draw plenty of stars and circles onto the smooth side of the fabric iron-on adhesive using the soft pencil. Then roughly cut out the shapes, leaving a narrow margin around the edge of the pencilled lines.

VARIATIONS

In addition to the stars and circles, cut out crescent moons; or perhaps go for something quite different like a series of naive animals - perhaps a whole Noah's ark?

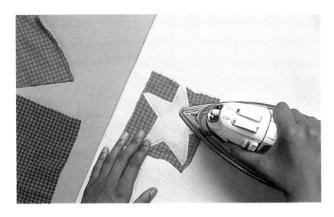

2 Lay down the rough side of each fabric iron-on adhesive cutout onto the reverse side of a piece of gingham material. (To make so many diverse shades of gingham, I dyed lengths of gingham fabric with different colours.) With your iron on a medium setting, iron over the paper to transfer the adhesive onto the fabric.

3 Cut around each of the stars and circles accurately, using sharp scissors so that the outline is very clear. You are now ready to begin decorating your blind.

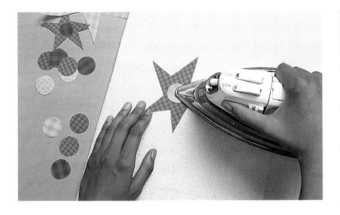

4 Choose which circles you want to go on which stars. Then remove the backing paper from the circle, position the circle in the centre of the star and iron down until it is firmly stuck in place.

5 Remove the backing paper from the star, place onto the blind and iron down in the same way. Repeat steps 4 and 5 until the blind is covered with randomly placed stars, circles and circles, on stars.

6 To make a border, take some extra circles and then iron them onto the lower edge of the blind. Either repeat the colours in a sequence or stick them down in randomly; the choice is yours.

GIFTS FOR THE HOME GALLERY

Lampshades

Globe artichokes and red tomatoes have been simply cut out and evenly arranged around a lampshade with green edging to make a very stylish accessory.

Floral tray (right)

The tray has been sanded down and sprayed gold. The cream, white and yellow flower scraps were then chosen to complement both the gold and green of the background.

Kitchen scales

These old-fashioned kitchen scales were rubbed down with wet and dry paper prior to painting and covering with decoupage.

Glass biscuit barrel

The scraps of fruit stuck onto the inside of this barrel were sealed with a coat of PVA glue and then coated with two coats of pale green emulsion paint and finally a coat of dark green emulsion.

Storage jars

Even storage jars can be made to look more interesting by covering them with decoupage. The chillies on this jar were colour photocopied and reduced to fit. Because you can see through the glass, the back of each motif is decorated to look the same as the front.

Napkin rings

For a fruit and flower theme, I cut out pictures of berries and
leaves and used these to decoupage some napkin rings
which were then given several coats of polyurethane varnish.

Salad bowl

An old salad bowl has been rejuvenated with coats
of varnish and vegetables have been added in
layers to give depth to the composition.

GIFTS FOR
SPECIAL OCCASIONS

Special occasions often mean buying presents, be it Mother's day or Easter, Christmas, or someone moving house. It can be difficult to buy something original which isn't going to break the bank, but with the aid of decoupage it is easy to dress up an object. In this chapter, some plain wooden hooks have been decorated with an Eastern European motif so that they look very decorative and original. Likewise, I have decorated a lampshade and hat box, made some cards and added decoupage to cardboard Easter eggs.

BLACK CAT
LAMP AND SHADE

Black cats silhouetted against a cream shade make a wonderful catty gift. Tall, stately Egyption cats, prowling fierce cats, and cosy, snuggling cats will all sit very happily side by side, united in their blackness.

1 Either photocopy or trace the cat silhouettes given on page 78, transfer the images onto the black sugar paper and then cut out as many of each shape of cat as you need, using either the scissors or craft knife.

VARIATIONS

The cats needn't just be black. Perhaps you would like to recreate your own cat, if you have one, or a series of differently coloured felines. All you need to do is cut out the cat in the correctly coloured sugar paper, or paint its markings over the top of the black paper.

2 Using the re-usable adhesive, arrange the silhouettes around the bottom edge of the lampshade grouping them in whichever way you prefer. When you are happy with your design it is time to move onto step 3.

3 One by one, stick the cats in place using the PVA glue. To make sure they are stuck firmly, rub your fingers lightly over the top of each one to remove any air bubbles.

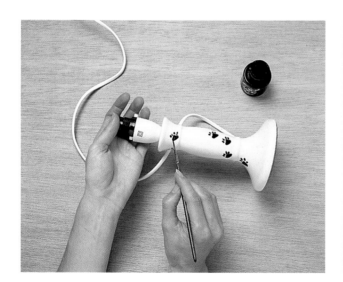

4 Using the chinagraph pencil, copy the paw prints that appear above onto the lamp base. With a chinagraph you can easily remove any mistakes you might make by simply rubbing off the marks. When the prints look right, fill in the design using the fine paintbrush and black acrylic paint.

5 To finish off the lamp base, wait until the acrylic paint has dried and then apply one or two coats of varnish to prevent the acrylic from chipping. Wait for the first coat of varnish to dry before applying the next.

EASTER KEY CUPBOARD

With the use of photographs of geese taken from a magazine and some fine chicken wire, the front of this key cupboard has been made to look just like a geese pen. For that special Easter touch, eggs have been stuck all around the edge of the cupboard.

1 Paint the entire key cupboard with two coats of the soft pink emulsion. Wait for the first coat of paint to thoroughly dry before applying the second coat.

YOU WILL NEED

Key cupboard

Emulsion paint (soft pink)

Paintbrush

Scissors

Pictures of geese and lots of eggs

Re-usable adhesive

PVA glue

Polyurethane matt wood varnish

Small piece of chicken wire

— VARIATIONS —

If pictures of geese don't readily come to hand, search out some brightly coloured ducks who are equally prolific egg layers, or even some hens with fluffy chicks.

2 Cut out the geese, trimming them as necessary so that they fit onto the cupboard door. Also cut out a selection of Easter eggs — these can usually be found in magazines around Easter time, of course!

3 Arrange the geese and the eggs around the cupboard, using the re-usable adhesive so that you can re-arrange them if you wish to. Keep aside one of the large pictures of a goose.

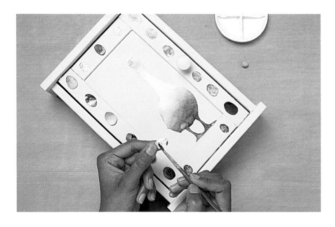

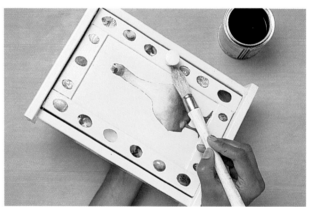

4 Once you have arranged the composition so that you like it, stick down the pictures with the PVA. Smooth down each picture with your fingers to remove any air bubbles.

5 Once the glue has dried, varnish the front of the cupboard with the polyurethane matt varnish. Use three to four coats allowing each one to dry before applying the next.

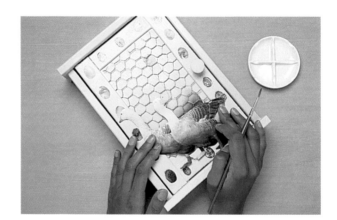

6 Take a piece of the chicken wire and cut it so that it is just slightly larger that the edges of the door. Then prise the edges of the chicken wire into the door frame, taking care not to damage the paintwork. Take the last goose and stick it over the bottom half of the wire.

HOUSEWARMING WOODEN HOOKS

A nice way to enliven some plain wooden hanging hooks is to decoupage them to complement just about anything in your home. A matching pair in similar colours makes a lovely housewarming present.

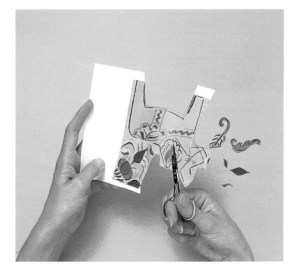

1 The patterns used for this decoupaged piece were taken from a postcard, which was colour copied, and the symbols were carefully cut out. Alternatively, if you can't get to a colour photocopier, you can thin the card by peeling off its back. To do this, dampen the back and then prise your nail into the middle of the card thickness and peel layers off.

YOU WILL NEED

Postcard
Access to a colour photocopier (optional)
Set of wooden hooks
Emulsion paint (sky blue)
Re-usable adhesive
Paintbrush
Scissors/craft knife
PVA glue
Polyurethane wood varnish

— VARIATIONS —

For a more personalized touch look for decorative letters in magazines or on wrapping paper or postcards and cut out and stick down the appropriate initials for each member of the household where the hooks will hang.

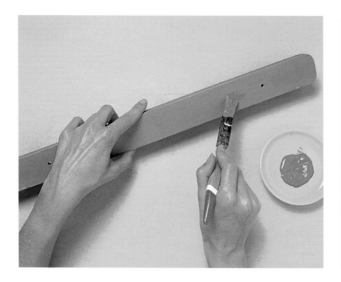

2 Paint the whole of the wooden hooks with a paint to complement the colours in the decoupage images. Here sky blue emulsion is used.

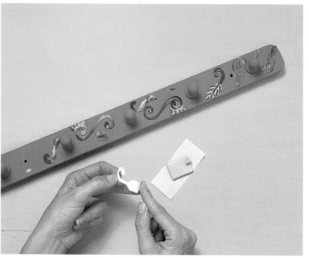

3 Using the re-usable adhesive, arrange the cut out patterns around the hooks, until you find a composition that you are happy with. Then it is time to move onto the next step.

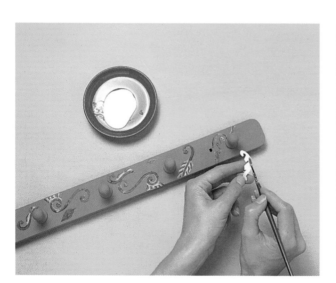

4 Stick down each motif with PVA glue, being careful not to tear the smaller pieces when they are being glued. Carefully rub a finger over each piece to remove any air bubbles that may be stuck behind.

5 Varnish the completed wooden hooks with polyurethane matt wood varnish, using as many coats as you wish. Allow the varnish to dry thoroughly in between coats.

GIFTS FOR SPECIAL OCCASIONS GALLERY

Mother's day card (below)
This Mother's day card uses flowers taken from an old greetings card, rearranged into a beautiful bouquet. Acrylics have been used to add details around the edge.

Papier mâché box
A round papier mâché box of humble origins is made to look special with the addition of a cut out and antiqued doily.

Photograph album
An inexpensive photograph album is given a new lease of life by being decorated. The images are packed closely together to make a very full picture on the surface of the album.

Valentine ca
This card
been m
by spong
white
turquoise b
Pieces of g
sprayed doily
then cut out
stuck in an oval,
which a cherub
been positio

Hat box
For a nostalgic air, paint a hat box in a rich deep green and then decorate it with a mixture of Victorian cutouts, including ladies, flowers and hands.

Christmas card
Cut out Victorian-style scraps of Santa Claus and arrange them on a card with pieces of gold-sprayed doily.

Valentine box
Gold sprayed paper cut to a heart shape and decorated with detailed cutouts makes the perfect Valentine box decoration.

Easter eggs
Cardboard eggs can be decorated to your own design by cutting out small-scale flowers and butterflies and sticking them over the egg.

49

GIFTS FOR CHILDREN

Decoupage can be used to decorate all kinds of children's possessions, ranging from furniture such as a cot, chair or cupboard to toys, containers and stationery. Children particularly like brightly coloured objects, so choose primary colours. Toy motifs which come on wrapping paper or from cutting up toy catalogues or baby magazines are ideal. Or you can always cut your own motifs as we have done in the butterfly wall frieze on pages 56-7 which uses brightly coloured gummed paper. Alternatively, use sticky-backed plastic to decorate. Draw the design on the paper backing and then cut out the motifs and stick into place on furniture, toys or plastic cutlery and plates.

KISSING DOVES DOLL'S CRIB

You don't necessarily need readily available images for decoupage, plain paper can be cut into pleasing shapes. A simple line drawing of a dove on doubled paper, when cut out and unfolded creates kissing doves which are a perfect size and shape for a doll's crib. To complete the doll's crib, slightly reduce the dove outline on a photocopier and make a piece of appliqué for the doll's cover featuring the doves as described on pages 36-7.

1 Paint the doll's crib in your child's favourite colour and using two to three coats of emulsion — here we used a bright red. For a smooth and even finish, leave the paint to dry in between coats.

YOU WILL NEED

Doll's crib
Emulsion paint (red)
Paintbrush
Dove outline (page 76)
Pencil
Tracing paper
Plain white paper
Scissors
Spray mount adhesive
PVA glue

— VARIATIONS —

In place of the kissing doves, you could cut out strings of girls and boys holding hands. To do this, fold a long strip of paper like a concertina so that each area of paper is the same width as you would like each girl or boy to be. Then draw the outline on the top piece and cut out the paper, remembering not to cut along their hands. Each child can then be individually decorated and the strips stuck in place along the sides of the crib, and shorter strips along the head- and footboards.

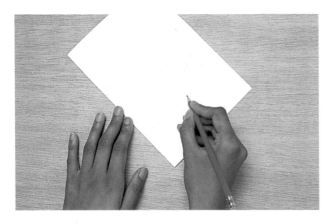

2 Trace the dove outline from page 76. Then fold a piece of plain white paper in half. Starting at the fold and beginning with the beak on the edge of the fold, transfer the dove's outline onto the paper. Do this by drawing thickly over the dove outline on the back of the tracing paper, position the tracing on the plain white paper and then drawing over the top once more.

3 Cut out the dove, being careful not to cut completely around the beak at the fold. This is where the doves join together so that they will eventually look as though they are kissing each other.

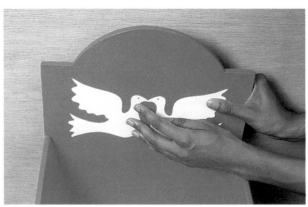

4 Unfold the paper to reveal the kissing doves and lay them out flat on your worksurface. Repeat steps 2 and 3 to make four large pairs and one small pair. The larger ones are for the outsides of the crib and the smaller one is for the headboard.

5 Spray mount the doves into position. By using spray mount you can quickly re-adjust the doves' position if you wish to. Smooth out any air bubbles that you come across.

6 Varnish the crib all over using PVA glue. Apply several coats, allowing each one to dry before painting the next, to give a good strong finish. Don't use wood varnish because it will discolour the white paper.

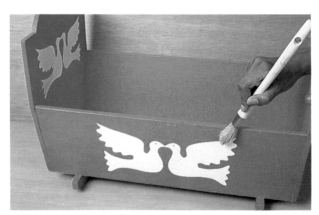

TOY BOX

Kids will love this brightly coloured toy box, decoupaged with toys cut out from various catalogues. The pictures make the box a label in itself: you don't have to open it up to see what is inside. For a more personalized toy box, cut out the child's name from brightly coloured gummed squares or patterned gift wrap. Draw the letter outlines first so that you know they are all the same size.

1 Paint the box sides alternately yellow and orange, and do the same with the box lid. Paint two to three coats leaving each coat to dry before applying the next to make the finish nicely smooth.

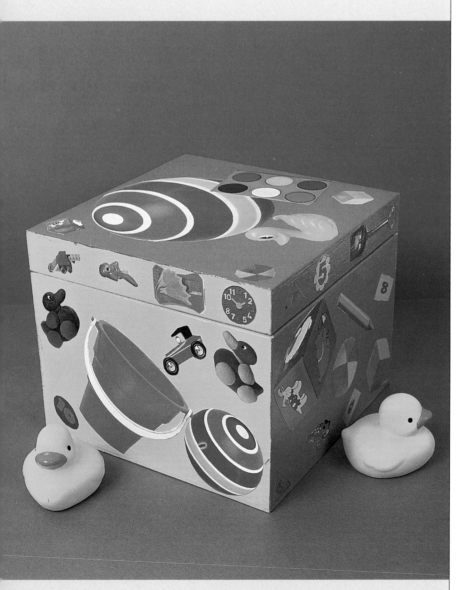

YOU WILL NEED

Square wooden box with lid

Emulsion paints (orange, yellow)

Paintbrush

Pictures of toys

Scissors

Re-usable adhesive

PVA glue

Polyurethane wood varnish

VARIATIONS

Instead of scattering the motifs all over the sides, why not build them up from the bottom edges so that it looks as though the toys are piled up high inside.

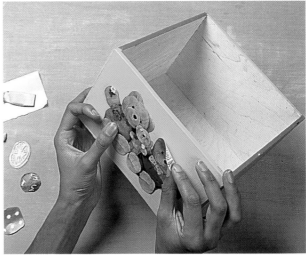

2 Cut out some pictures of brightly coloured toys from magazines or catalogues. Make sure that you have a mixture of sizes — the border of the lid, for example, will need smaller pictures, while the sides can take larger toys.

3 Arrange the pictures around the box and its lid, using the re-usable adhesive. In this way, you can re-adjust the pictures until you have designed a composition that you are happy with.

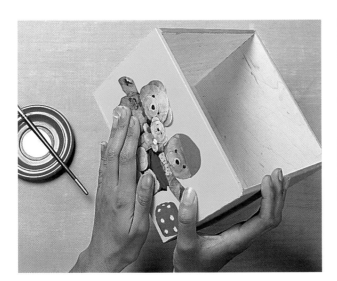

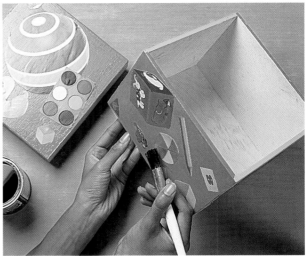

4 Stick the pictures in position using the PVA glue and smooth out any air bubbles with your fingers so that the images are well attached.

5 Varnish the entire box and lid with the polyurethane varnish. Give it three to four coats allowing each one to dry before applying the next so that the end result is tough and durable.

BUTTERFLY FRIEZE

This charming frieze is made very simply using brightly coloured sticky paper squares. The shapes are cut out using outlines given at the back of this book and then they can, of course, be stuck in place very easily. Mix together all the brightest colours to make a most exotic species of butterfly. Vary the sizes of the butterflies, too, so that you have some large ones and some small ones.

1 Water down the blue paint and wash the border using a fat paintbrush in a circular motion to create the cloudy effect shown in the photograph above.

YOU WILL NEED

Watercolour paint (blue)

Paintbrush

20 cm (8 in)-wide border paper

Butterfly templates (page 77)

Tracing paper

Pencil

Brightly coloured gummed paper

Scissors

Re-usable adhesive

Varnish

— VARIATIONS —

These gummed paper squares come in so many bright colours that you can create any picture you want in this way. Piles of different kinds of fruit, the sky at night, teddy bears in all manner of poses — let your imagination run riot and you will soon be filling friezes with an endless variety of designs.

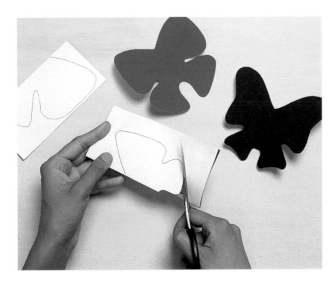

2 Trace the templates on page 77. Then fold your gummed paper in half, transfer the template outlines onto the back of the paper and cut out to give two wings of exactly the same size. To transfer the outline, draw thickly over the butterfly outline on the back of the tracing paper, position the tracing on the folded gummed paper and then draw over the top once more.

3 In contrasting colours, make the butterfly bodies and wing patterns in exactly the same way as for the butterfly wings described in step 2.

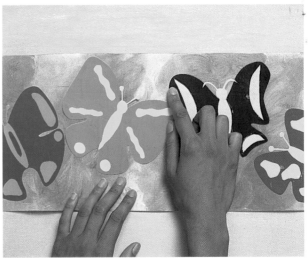

4 Dampen the bodies and wing patterns with a little water and attach onto the wings mixing the colours as much as you like to make sure you end up with beautifully ornate butterflies.

5 Now arrange the completed butterflies onto the cloudy frieze using re-usable adhesive to position them. Once they are flying around to your liking stick them down and then cover with a coat of protective varnish; either matt or glossy.

GIFTS FOR CHILDREN GALLERY

Shelf unit

These shelves looked a little tired so it has been repainted and decorated with a series of fifties-style images.

Pretend play (middle)

A child's clear plastic bag and picnic set have been decorated using sticky-backed plastic cut into flower shapes.

Storage containers

A shoe box and folder (opposite) are both given new life by painting them and then decorating them with simple geometric cut outs.

Decorative plates

Plates such as these can be expensive, but with a
touch of emulsion paint and decoupage they
can quickly be decorated to fit in
with the decor of a
child's room.

Wastepaper bins

Catering-size drinking chocolate drums have been converted
into bins for children's rooms: one with bold brash roses and
the other with nursery rhyme characters.

GIFTS FOR ADULTS

As you will see from some of the projects in this
chapter, even the smallest item can be covered in
decoupage, such as a window wedge or a trinket
box. One of the techniques included in this section is
sticking the motif to the inside of a glass container
and then painting on top so that the image shines out
of a painted interior. This is a popular technique in
France. Alternatively, decoupage a wooden clock
which is an easy item to work on: cut your own
circle from MDF, drill a hole in the centre, affix
a quartz mechanism, and then decoupage
the clock face.

ANGELS GLASS TRINKET BOX

This pretty little box is an ideal gift to hold small pieces of jewellery. The technique used here is to stick the pictures inside the box, face down on the glass and then paint behind the images inside the box so that the box has a lustre.

1 Select the angels from a decoupage set, making sure that they are small enough to fit onto the sides of the box. Cut them out carefully, and trim off any excess background.

YOU WILL NEED

Angel images

Small glass trinket box

Embroidery scissors

Re-usable adhesive

PVA glue

Paintbrush (fine)

Soft cloth

Emulsion paint (mauve)

VARIATIONS

Instead of these little angels, look for small pictures of shells, say, or flowers. If you are making this box as a gift for a friend, use images that you know are a particular favourite.

2 Arrange the angels face down on the insides of the box, so that they can be seen when you look at the outside of the box. Use re-usable adhesive at first, so that you can adjust them to your liking.

3 Stick the angels into the positions you have chosen, using the PVA adhesive and pressing them down firmly. Push out the excess glue and air bubbles by wiping over them with the soft cloth from the centre of the image outwards.

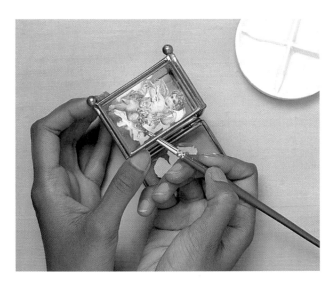

4 Paint the insides of the trinket box and over the angels with a thin coat of PVA adhesive to seal the pictures. Allow the PVA to dry until it is only very slightly tacky.

5 Now, paint the insides of the box with the emulsion paint. Because both the PVA and the emulsion are water-based, the tacky PVA will mix with the emulsion paint and give the sides of the box a cloudy look. Allow this to dry and then seal with another coat of PVA.

PINEAPPLE WINDOW WEDGE

Even the smallest things can be covered with decoupage to good effect. This delicate window wedge has a pineapple carved onto its handle, so the theme has been carried through by sticking a pineapple onto its body.

1 If you can't find a picture of a pineapple that is small enough to fit onto your window wedge, colour copy any one that you can find and reduce it to fit. Most copy shops have colour photocopiers.

YOU WILL NEED

Window wedge
Picture of a pineapple
Colour photocopier
Manicure scissors/craft knife
Re-usable adhesive
PVA glue
Polyurethane wood varnish
Paintbrush

TIP

You will quite likely find window wedges with all sorts of other designs on their ends. Whatever you choose, try to find a motif that reflects the wedge's design, and this will make the end result a very pleasing object.

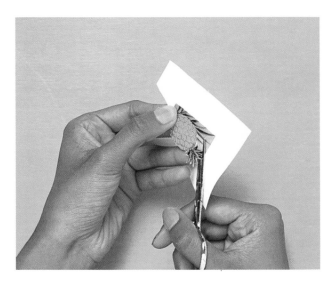

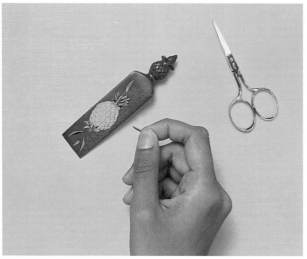

2 Carefully cut out the pineapple using either the manicure scissors or the craft knife and if there is any extra foliage in the picture cut that out as well for added interest.

3 Arrange the pictures into position before you stick them down. Use re-usable adhesive to keep them in place so that you can see how the finished design will look before you stick the pieces in place.

4 Stick down the images being careful not to tear the tiny pieces when they are damp with the PVA. Press down firmly and carefully smooth out the air bubbles with your finger tips.

5 Varnish all of the window wedge with six to seven coats of polyurethane varnish to give a highly glossed and even finish.

GIFTS FOR ADULTS GALLERY

Wall frieze
This frieze has been made by cutting out and sticking down squares of sticky-backed fake suede onto lining paper.

Pencil pot
Rather a dull pot, I painted it gold and then covered it with decoupage of gold script printed on tracing paper.

Book cover
This book has been treated to music stained with a tea bag. Musical instruments have been pasted on top before varnishing.

Wooden clock

A wooden clock kit has been decorated with overlapping gold cut outs of clocks which are printed on translucent paper.

Mirror frame

This mock tortoiseshell mirror, a junk shop find, has been embellished by cut-outs of harps chosen because of their complementary colouring.

Candle shades

These are easy to make and great to give away as a present. This one is decorated with decoupaged squares of sticky-backed fake suede.

Trinket box

A small round box is a good place to keep cufflinks. This one has been painted black and the border around the lid edge has been made from scraps of paper. The crown was cut out from a magazine.

FRAMES

Picture and mirror frames, especially wide ones, make good surfaces on which to decoupage. Buy them off the shelf or look out for them in thrift shops and boot fairs. They can be completely smothered in abstract images, such as the yellow geometric frame on pages 74-5. Or give them a colour wash so that the grain of the wood shows through and they can then be decorated with a lingering line of vine and torn paper leaves. Frames can reflect the interest of the owner, whether it be cars or cats, and patterns may be applied in a regimented fashion, or dotted about with plenty of space between each.

CATS FRAME

This frame illustrates how a picture can be built up in steps from images cut out of wrapping paper. The cat images symmetrically surround the whole of the frame, making it the purrfect frame in which to place pictures of your favourite pet.

This second-hand frame was quite scratched and so we first sanded it down and painted it to create a smoother surface on which to work. Always take great care to smooth down the images well as you stick them down to ensure no glue bubbles form.

1 Cut out lots of cats from the wrapping paper, making sure that they are small enough to fit around the frame. You may not be able to find paper exactly like this one, but there are many other commercially available gift wrapping papers with images of cats on them.

YOU WILL NEED

Gift wrapping paper

Manicure scissors/craft knife

Re-usable adhesive

Picture frame

PVA glue

Paintbrush

—— VARIATIONS ——

If you are lucky enough to find a wrapping paper with cats in many different poses then you can create a more informal design on your picture frame. Scatter them around the frame always using re-usable adhesive because then you can safely keep on repositioning them until you know that you are happy with the design.

2 Using re-usable adhesive as a temporary adhesive, arrange the cats around the frame. You can place them around randomly, but a symmetric pattern like this works very well.

3 Also using small pieces of the re-usable adhesive, place the larger cats in each corner of the frame. Position them so that they face inwards and at an angle across the mitring.

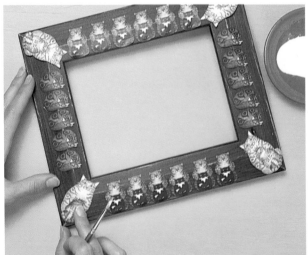

4 Place a smaller cat on top of each larger cat, so that it looks like they are sitting in front of them. Make sure that they are both sitting on the 'ground' or the cats will look slightly strange, as though one of them were floating in the air.

5 Stick down all the cats with PVA glue and once they are secured and the glue dried, varnish over the frame also with the PVA glue. When you first apply it, it will be white and opaque, but it will dry to a transparent finish. Two to three coats will suffice.

TORN PAPER LEAVES FRAME

This frame involves decorative painting as well as decoupage. Again, you don't necessarily need to use images that are available, you can just as easily create your own. Here leaves are made by tearing gummed paper into tiny leaves.

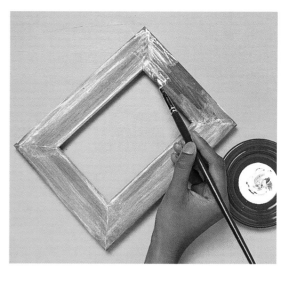

1 Sand the wooden picture frame all over to prepare it for painting. This will roughen the surface so that it will accept a water-based paint wash. Then mix the white paint 1:1 with water and paint on the frame. The grain of the wood will show through the white paint quite clearly.

VARIATIONS

In place of the leaves, perhaps you would like to make tiny bunches of grapes, say, or just hang pairs of cherries all the way around its edge. Using the same principal, tear tiny circles of paper in the appropriate colour and stick them in place grouping them closely for the grapes, or suspending the cherries from previously hand-painted stalks.

2 Rip plenty of tiny leaf-like shapes from the green gummed paper. As the paper is white on one side, when the leaves are torn, a white edge is created, giving the leaves some depth.

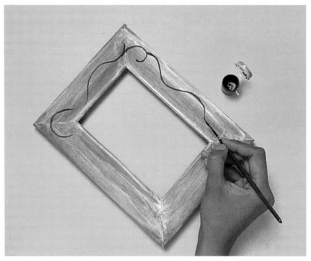

3 Using the fine paintbrush, paint a green curvy line around two sides of the frame — the top or bottom and one of the edges — with little branches coming off the main line.

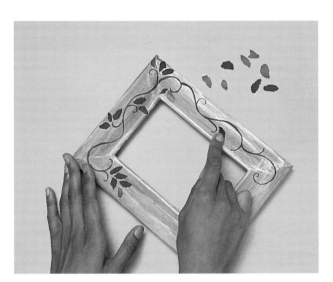

4 Dampen the back of the paper leaves and secure them to the ends of the branches. Group them together in clusters, as on a tree, varying the numbers of leaves in each one to keep the design looking fluid.

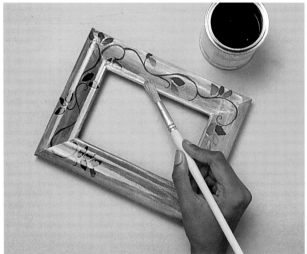

5 Varnish all over the picture frame with several coats of the polyurethane satin varnish to give a shiny finish. Allow each coat to dry thoroughly before applying the next layer.

FRAMES GALLERY

Victorian frame

To make a Victorian style frame, a square wooden frame has been painted with blue emulsion and scraps have been stuck onto the top as a collage.

Vintage car frame

For the lover of old cars, a frame decorated with vintage cars is appropriate. These images have been copied on a photocopier and then hand tinted before being stuck onto the frame and varnished.

Calligraphic frame

A plain frame has been decoupaged using torn paper with golden calligraphy and star sequins. It was then varnished with three coats of polyurethane varnish.

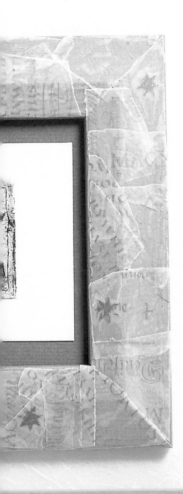

Strawberry frame

This black frame was rubbed with gold wax and then decorated with strawberries cut out of magazines. The red and green of the strawberries contrast well with the black and gold.

Tartan frame

This dramatic, tartan-covered frame has been dressed up still further with three silver fish and some hand-coloured Victorian engravings.

Mosaic frame

The best decoupaged frames are those which are quite wide and allow enough room to make a bold statement. A yellow frame has been decorated in a mosaic style by cutting out shapes in complementary colours and sticking them over the frame.

TEMPLATES

Use the templates on these pages either as they appear, or enlarge or reduce them on a photocopier should you wish to alter their size. To transfer an outline, trace over the shape using a soft pencil on tracing paper. Go over the back of the outline with the pencil and then position the outline onto the paper from which you will be cutting the shape. Hold it firmly in place and draw over the top of the outline one more time. To make a long-lasting template for repeated use, transfer the outline onto cardboard.

Kissing doves doll's crib
(see page 52)

Butterfly frieze
(see page 56)

*Stars and circles
roller blind*
(see page 36)

Black cat lamp and shade
(see page 42)

USEFUL ADDRESSES

UNITED KINGDOM

AB Woodworking
Unit J, Peulre Wen
Gobowen
Oswestry
Shropshire SY10 7JZ
Tel: 01691 670425
(extensive range of boxes
available through mail
order; catalogue £2,
refundable with first order;
trade enquiries welcome)

Fred Aldous Ltd.
PO Box 37
Lever Street
Manchester 1
M60 1UX
Tel: 0161 236 2477
(fish transfers, decoupage
varnish and items upon
which to decoupage)

Art & Craft
1 Althorp Close
Wellingborough
Northants NN8 5FE

Attic Window
34 High Street
Innerleithen
Peebleshire
Scotland EH44 6HF
Tel: 01896 831140

Binney and Smith
(Europe) Ltd
Ampthill Road
Bedford MK42 9RS
Tel: 01234 360201
(liquitex acrylic paint,
gesso and paintbrushes)

Craft Creation Limited
Unit 9 Harpers Yard
Ruskin Road
Tottenham
London N17 8NE
Tel: 0181 885 2655

Decorative Arts
Company
Basement
5A Royal Crescent
London W11 4SL
Tel: 0171 371 4303
(range of papier mâché
items available for
decoration; mail order)

The Dover Bookshop
18 Earlham Street
London WC2H 9LN
Tel: 0171 836 2111

Falkiner Fine Papers Ltd.
76 Southampton Row
London WC1B 4AR
Tel: 0171 831 1151

General Trading
Company Ltd.
144 Sloane Street
London SW1X 9BL
Tel: 0171 730 0411

Global Village
17 St James Street
South Petherton
Somerset TA13 5BS
Tel: 01460 41166

Hamleys
188-196 Regent Street
London W1R 6BT
Tel: 0171 734 3161

Hawkin & Co.
Saint Margaret
Harleston
Norfolk IP20 0PJ
Tel: 01986 82536

Karin Van Heerden
PO Box 558
Oxford OX1 5AJ
(cat papers as used on page
70, available by mail order)

Mamelock Press Ltd.
Northen Way
Bury St Edmund
Suffolk IP32 6NJ
Tel: 01284 762291

Ornamenta
PO Box 786
London SW7 2TG
Tel: 0171 584 3857

Panduro Hobby Ltd.
West Way House
Transport Avenue
Brentford
Middlesex TW8 9HF
Tel: 0181 847 6161

Paperchase
213 Tottenham Court Rd.
London W1P 9AF
Tel: 0171 437 2476
(decorative papers)

Philip and Tacey
Northway
Andover
Hampshire SP10 5BA
Tel: 01264 332171
(crackle and patinating
varnish)

Polyvine Ltd.
Vine House
Rockhampton
Berkeley
Glos. GL13 9DT
Tel: 01454 261276
(crackle glaze, crackle
varnish, and a variety of
other decorative paint
finishes)

Reeves Dryad
178 Kensington High St.
London W8 7XH
Tel: 0171 937 5370

Rob Jackson
28 Culme Road
West Derby
Liverpool L12 7HL

AUSTRALIA

Burwood Craft Centre
173 Burwood Road
Burwood NSW 2134
Tel: (02) 747 5714
Fax: (02) 747 5654

Cottage Road Gifts and
Crafts
514 Goodwood Road
Daw Park
South Australia 5041
Tel: (08) 271 0100

Craft Crowd, The
Shop 60 Sunnybank
Plaza
Main Road
Sunnybank
Queensland 44109
Tel: (07) 345 9812

Crafty
7 Dickson Street
Wooloowin
Queensland 4030
Tel: (02) 357 5393

Hobbytex
5 Victoria Avenue
Castle Hill NSW 2154
Tel: (02) 634 5388
Fax: (02) 899 1026

Queensland Handcrafts
6 Manning Street
South Brisbane
Queensland 4101
Tel: (07) 844 5722
Fax: (07) 844 5501

Rosenhain, Lipmanns &
Peers Pty.
147 Burnley Street
Richmond
Melbourne
Victoria 3121
Tel: (03) 428 1485

NEW ZEALAND

Auckland Folk Art
Centre
591 Remuera Rd
Upland Village
Auckland
Tel: (09) 524 0936

Dominion Paint Centre
227 Dominion Rd
Mt Eden
Tel: (09) 638 7593

The Partners
St Martins Stationary
5 Austin-Kirk Lane
Christchurch 2

SOUTH AFRICA

Anne's Arts and Crafts
6 Recreation Rd
Fish Hoek
Cape Town
Tel: (021) 782 2061

Art, Leather and
Handcraft Specialist
Shop 6 Musgrave Centre
124 Musgrave Road
Durban
Tel: (031) 21 9517

Art Mates
Shop 313 Musgrave
Centre
124 Musgrave Road
Durban
Tel: (031) 21 0094

Crafty Suppliers
32 Main Road
Claremont
Cape Town
Tel: (021) 61 0286

Craftsman, The
Shop 10 Progress House
110 Bordeaux Drive
Randburg
Johannesburg
Tel: (011) 787 1846

E. Schweikerdt (Pty) Ltd.
Vatika Centre
Cnr Muckleneuk and
Fehrsen Street
Brooklyn
Pretoria
Tel: (012) 45 5406

Franken
445 Hilda Street
Hatfield
Pretoria
Tel: (011) 43 6414

L & P Stationery and
Artists' Requirements
65b Church Street
Bloemfontein
Tel: (051) 30 3061

Mycrafts Shop (Pty)
Aliwal Street
Bloemfontein
Tel: (051) 48 4119

Peers Handicrafts
35 Burg Street
Cape Town
Tel: (021) 24 2520

PW Story (Pty) Ltd.
18 Foundry Lane
Durban
Tel: (031) 306 1224

Southern Arts and Crafts
105 Main Street
Rosettenville
Johannesburg
Tel: (011) 683 6566

INDEX